THE POWER OF GRATITUDE

The writing of this book was given to me by the grace of God. It is now my privilege to pass it on to you as a gift, free of any charge or obligation. It would, however, give me great pleasure for you to make a donation of any amount to one of the following four worthy causes:

- Eastern Pregnancy Information Clinic
  P.O. Box 1838, Kinston, NC 28502
- The GATE of Kinston
  P.O. Box 638, Kinston, NC 28502
- Son Set Ministries (for The Refuge)
  P.O. Box 5247, Kinston, NC 28503-5247
- The Salvation Army (for use in Kinston, NC)
  P.O. Box 1479, Kinston, NC 28503-1479

DAN E. PERRY, ATTORNEY
P.O. BOX 1475 | KINSTON, NC 28503-1475

ALSO BY DAN E. PERRY

More Than I Deserve, 2007

The Game of Life . . . and How to Play It, 2008

My Greatest Discovery . . . Christ in You, the Hope of Glory, 2009

101 Quirks, Quips, and Quotes, 2010

God's Amazing Love Letter . . . and Its Impact on America, 2010

THE POWER SERIES

The Power of Letting . . . Letting God Live in and through You, 2011

The Power of Humility . . . Letting Go of Self-Pride, 2011

THE POWER SERIES

THE POWER OF GRATITUDE

Letting Gratefulness Be Your Lifestyle

Dan E. Perry

CHAPEL HILL
PRESS, INC.®

Back cover image by Michael Taylor, photographer,
Williamson's Photography, Kinston, NC.

All Bible verses from New King James Version, except where
New Living Translation (NLT) or other versions are referenced.
Italics in Scripture quotations are the author's emphasis.

ISBN 978-1-59715-082-8

First Printing

DEDICATION

The dedication of this book was an easy choice:

First, it has to be dedicated to the Holy Spirit, who led me every step of the way—at least to the extent I allowed Him. Anything that is off-base and not right is of my own personal doing, and not that of the indwelling Holy Spirit.

Second, it has to be dedicated to my dear wife, Margaret, who is and has been my chief editor and constructive critic for this and all my previous books. As my best friend and prayer partner, she shares with me her insight and spiritual wisdom, as well as her prayers, on a daily basis. She is the one human being for whom I am most thankful for everything!

CONTENTS

ACKNOWLEDGMENTS

When I thought of acknowledging those who helped in the writing of this book on gratitude, the word "gratitude" itself came to mind. For whom am I most thankful? In addition to the Holy Spirit and Margaret, I am thankful for:

Barbara Ruth Perry, Lina Gibbs, and Rob McArthur for their time and effort in reviewing the prepublished manuscript for theological correctness. Their thoughts and suggestions are very much appreciated.

Katie Severa as graphic designer, and Edwina Woodbury as publisher, for their excellent cooperative work in putting together the final product.

Linda Murray, who was responsible for interpreting and typing my scribblings to put in final form to present to the publisher.

And finally, I'm thankful to you, dear reader, for your endurance, support, and encouragement.

"Thank you." Those two words are probably the first combination of words we learn as infants. After "Da-da" and "Ma-ma," then comes "please." We want our children to be good little boys and girls, so we start with the basics. When someone gives them a lollipop or compliments their pretty hair, our immediate response as parents is, "Say 'thank you.'" After being drilled enough they should begin to get the idea, but we still have to remind them with the familiar, "What do you say?" or "What do you say when someone gives you something?" When that doesn't work, we continue our instructions by putting the words in their mouth: "Say 'thank you.'" Finally, after several years of intense training, their little minds begin to catch on to the concept of gratitude. It's a proud moment when parents hear for the first time their five-, six-, or seven-year-old respond with an unassisted "thank you." But just when we think they're beginning to get the picture, our balloon pops on the very next occasion! We are forced to go back to square one with, "What do you say?" followed in the next breath with, "Say "thank you.'"

The purpose of that little scenario is to remind us that gratitude is not only something to be learned but it is a choice we make. Young parents want their children to learn that "thank you" should be a natural response that is basic to their general makeup, and should be carried over into adulthood.

My purpose and overall objective in writing this book is to help us all see the need and value of going beyond the elementary idea that gratitude means being thankful *for something*. When we begin to understand the fullness of gratitude and explore its scope and dimension, we move beyond that elementary stage and discover that true gratitude opens the door to the very presence of God. We begin to catch a glimpse of the transforming power of gratitude and what in-depth gratitude is all about.

There are basically only two kinds of people in this world: a believer and an unbeliever in Jesus Christ. If you, dear reader, claim to be a believer, I pray that this book will lead you to a closer walk with Him and a clearer understanding of who you are in Christ. If you are an unbeliever, I pray the Holy Spirit will use this book to draw you to make a decision to accept.

Jesus as the Christ, the Son of the living God, and your personal Lord and Savior.

PART ONE

Responding to God with Gratitude and Praise

CHAPTER I

What Is Gratitude All About?

Defining Gratitude

One of the best definitions of "gratitude" I ever heard was given by Nancy Leigh DeMoss in her classic book, *Choosing Gratitude*. She wrote, "Gratitude is learning to recognize and express appreciation for the benefits we have received from God and from others." From that definition let's analyze what we are trying to learn about gratitude:

Learning to recognize what we receive each day means our minds and hearts need to be constantly open, alert, and on the lookout to be aware of the many blessings that come our way each day. It's like making every day a treasure hunt for blessings.

And to express appreciation... After we become aware of our blessings, we should make a conscious effort to thank God for the blessings He provides. It's a matter of disciplining ourselves to respond with appropriate gratitude to what He has given us.

For the benefits we have received from God... Our heavenly Father is continually showering us with benefits in the form of good things. The good news is that even the "bad things" He allows in our lives are technically "benefits" He uses to make us more like His Son. That may seem hard to believe, but I'm convinced it's true if we respond to our adverse circumstances with a spirit of gratitude.

And from others. Not only does gratitude define us as people who value our relationship with God, but it also defines us in our relationships with other people around us.

If we have a genuine attitude of gratitude toward God and others we are humbly letting it be known that we are undeserving of any of our benefits and blessings.

Make Gratitude Our Lifestyle

Most of us are programmed to express thankfulness to people. But if we limit our gratitude merely to people, we are missing the true essence of what gratitude is all about. James makes it clear: "Every good gift and every perfect gift is from above, and comes down from the Father of lights" (James 1:17). If we are to develop an in-depth lifestyle of gratitude we must recognize that all our blessings come from God, for it is only through His grace and mercy that we experience any of the real joys of living. That is in no way to diminish the importance of our gratitude to others; rather, it's a simple matter of perspective and seeing the full picture of the essence of gratitude.

To make gratitude our lifestyle means that our whole being is focused on God and His goodness. It means that not only each day, but each minute of each day, our subconscious thoughts are tuned in to God and His sovereign plan for our lives. Even as I write those words, I'm telling myself, *But that's impossible! Nobody can be focused on God every minute of every day!* How true! How true that is! I can't do it, you can't do it, and nobody can do it.

But let me tell you what I'm learning—slowly but surely. Some of you are far more advanced than I am in being constantly aware of God's indwelling presence in your life as a believer. We know that when we receive Christ, God's Spirit takes up residence within us. He becomes central to our innermost being, but that fact alone does not prevent our minds from going off on a tangent from time to time. In our humanity Satan uses the world system and the flesh to divert our attention away from the Holy Center of our lives. In other words, our mind goes astray. What

I'm learning (or, I should say, *trying to learn*) is that the Lord is not alarmed by my inability to remain focused on Him. He's trying to teach me that each time my mind wanders, He gently calls me to bring my thoughts back to Him. As Sarah Young says, "The quickest way to redirect our mind to Him is to whisper His name—*Jesus.*"

So if we want to make gratitude our lifestyle, we need to stay focused on Jesus, through whom we come to know God. And if we really want to stay focused on Jesus, we must discipline ourselves to spend sufficient quality time in His presence.

Therein lies the secret of "learning to recognize and express appreciation for the benefits we have received from God and from others."

Being Thankful for God's Forgiveness

Oswald Chambers wrote, "The thing that awakens the deepest well of gratitude in a human being is that God has forgiven sin." That is such a profound and insightful statement, for it zeroes in on the very essence of what the gospel message is all about. God sent His Son into the world to be the means by which our sins can be forgiven. The central focus of our observance of Holy Communion, or the Lord's Supper, is forgiveness of sins. When we use the word "Eucharist" we are referring to Holy Communion and the blood sacrifice of Jesus. Eucharist embodies the highest act of thanksgiving for our ultimate blessing received from God: Jesus' death on the cross for the remission of our sins.

It has been said that *guilt*, *grace*, and *gratitude* are at the heart of the gospel. In a larger sense they tell the basic story of the whole Bible. Let's consider these three doctrines:

Guilt. Because we are descended from Adam,

we inherit his sin nature and will remain forever guilty and destined for eternal damnation unless a dramatic change takes place during our lifetime. It becomes a matter of paying our sin debt—a debt that we ourselves cannot pay.

Grace. Our hopeless status can be changed only by the undeserved grace of God. Because of His unconditional love for all mankind, He sent His only begotten Son into the world to pay our sin debt for us by shedding His blood on the cross. That's the good news: the gospel of Jesus Christ!

Gratitude. Our natural response to this good news is one of gratitude and thanksgiving for this incredible, undeserved gift from God. We are then led to shout it from the mountaintop as we give all praise and glory to our Lord and Savior! If we truly understand the full impact of what God has done for us, through the sacrificial offering of His Son, we cannot help but be motivated to rejoice in thanksgiving, praise, and holy worship of our sovereign God.

But the Gift Is Not Ours Unless We Receive It

The key to making any gift effective is that the recipient must accept it. And how do we receive God's gift of salvation for the forgiveness of our sins, thereby qualifying us for eternal life? It takes a simple act of repentance and faith. By repentance we are saying that we are truly sorry for all our sins and are willing to turn from them. Most of the time it's not easy to actually give up a sinful lifestyle—and that's where our faith and the power of the Holy Spirit come in.

When we confess our sins, and by faith ask Jesus Christ to forgive our transgressions, God comes into our lives in the form of the Holy Spirit and takes up permanent residence within our being. He wipes away all our sins and empowers us to live the life He designed us to live. That's God's gift to us—*if only we receive it!*

CHAPTER II

Gratitude Opens the Door to God's Presence

What is gratitude all about? We grew up thinking that the words "gratitude" and "thankfulness" were synonymous. They meant being grateful or thankful for something someone did for us. If we have a spirit of gratitude, we have a spirit of thanksgiving for our blessings. For example, we "ask the blessing" or "return thanks" before eating a meal in grateful appreciation for what God has provided for us.

If we think about it, we will realize that gratitude is the essential element of our praise and worship. When we offer our praise to God, we are thanking him for who He is—our Creator and sovereign God of the universe. And when we worship Him, we are thanking Him for awakening our consciousness to His holiness. This is all accomplished through a spirit of gratitude and thanksgiving.

What the Lord has been trying to teach me in all this is that if I am to know Him and understand what He wants me to know and do, I must approach Him with a spirit of gratitude. I must continually thank Him for who He is and what He has done for me.

If I am to be more like Jesus, I must "practice His presence" within me, for therein lies the means He uses to accomplish His purpose for my life.

In John 10:7 Jesus made it clear that He is the door through whom we come to know the Father. In her devotional book *Jesus Calling*, Sarah Young uses the image of a door to help us see the reality of all this.

She says it's like having a door between God and us through which we must enter to be in His presence.

The Door of Awareness

God's desire is that we choose to follow His leading to open the door. Upon deeper reflection I'm convinced that we should call it the *door of awareness* for the simple reason that God is already present in the lives of all believers. He came to indwell us when we accepted His Son as our Lord and Savior. It's our lack of awareness of His presence that needs to be overcome through understanding and application. When we finally wake up and discover the reality of the mystery of what Paul termed as "Christ in you, the hope of glory" (Colossians 1:27), we're on our way to opening wide the door of awareness of His indwelling presence in the form of the Holy Spirit.

There are a number of ways to open the door of awareness of God's indwelling presence, but I'm persuaded that one of the most effective ways is through a grateful attitude. Sarah Young writes, "Thankfulness is built on a structure of trust." She's exactly right, for if we seem to be reluctant or don't see the need to give thanks, we should check our foundation of trust by asking these questions: *Do I trust God in all things? Is He really in control of my life? Is disbelief standing in the way of my praise and thanksgiving for all He's done for me?* I'm convinced that when we have a spirit of thanksgiving flowing freely from our hearts and lips, God uses our attitude of gratitude to draw us closer to Him.

God wants all His children to know Him and live according to His will. His job is to lead. Our job is to follow. But for these objectives to be best accomplished, we must be aware of His indwelling presence. I'm persuaded that our awareness of His presence and His leading in our lives comes only through a close relationship with Him.

The more intimate we are in our relationship with God, the more aware we are of His leading.

The Fifth Dimension of Life

We've all heard of the four dimensions of life: the three dimensions of space—*height*, *width*, and *depth*—and the fourth is *time*. But let me suggest that there is even a fifth dimension to which most of us have given little thought, and that is the often-overlooked dimension of *awareness*. None of the other four have any meaning for our spiritual growth unless we are made aware of them. In fact, hardly anything in life has meaning unless we are aware of it! You may have heard of the example of the poor Texas farmer whose small farm was discovered after his death to be sitting on top of the richest oil field in the world. He was rich and didn't know it! He never became aware of what was his, just for the taking. We can apply that same principle to "Christ in you, the hope of glory." Oh, if only we were fully aware of the richness of the blessings within the life of every believer! They are there in abundance—if only we would take them and use them for His glory. What a blessing that would be—just waiting to be discovered!

But There's One Further Dimension

Before we can experience the lasting benefits and blessings of God's presence, we should go a step further and mention *openness*. The *dimension of openness* is crucial to becoming aware of God's presence. As we develop a genuine attitude of praise, thanksgiving, and worship of the Creator and Sustainer of life, we begin to establish this added dimension of openness, or we might say *receptivity*. This attitude of receptivity paves the way to our awareness of His presence within the life of every believer.

If you are an unbeliever, I pray that you will see the need for an open mind and an awareness of the blessings that are yours when you receive Christ in your life. This is not to be judgmental of any unbeliever. I'm merely stating what I believe to be true for anyone who makes the decision to accept Jesus as his or her Lord and Savior. That is not to say that, even against your will, God in His Providence can't knock you off your feet as He did with Saul in his Damascus road experience.

God uses our attitude of receptivity and openness to the gospel message to draw us unto Him and lead us to repentance, salvation, and eternal life.

CHAPTER III

The Four Levels of Gratitude

The various levels of thanksgiving and gratitude seem to be reflected in four distinct types of people:

1. *The Constant Complainer.* This is the lowest level, and we generally don't see a great many of these folks around. But occasionally we do run into such a person. He's the kind who has a negative attitude about everything. He follows Murphy's Law: "If anything is going to go wrong, it will go wrong." He has the attitude that "this is going to be a bad day—I just know it will. I'm not going to catch any fish, because I never do. I know I am going to miss this short putt, because I've just got a feeling." I used to complain

about my golf shots straying from the center of the fairway, or ending up about thirty feet from the pin instead of four feet for an easy birdie putt. I tend to be a perfectionist and want all my drives in the middle of the fairway and my approach shots within easy birdie range. We used to kid our golfing buddy, Ray Rouse, when he constantly complained about his golf game. Carlton Oliver would make the observation, "That man has never made a good golf shot in his life." Ray is really not all that bad, for most of us complain about not being as good as we'd like to be. But the Constant Complainer I'm talking about is the person who sees nothing good in anything, and therefore has no reason to be thankful for anything. That person is at the lowest level on the gratitude scale of one to ten. He's at zero, or maybe on a good day, he might reach a one.

2. *The Ingrate*. This person may move up the scale to a two or possibly a three on our gratitude scale. He's the person who doesn't do all that much complaining, but he just doesn't show much gratitude

in his everyday life. He doesn't complain about the weather; he just doesn't see the need to be thankful and express appreciation for the many good things about life. He fits in the category of "simple ingratitude." He's like the squirrel or the hog eating acorns under the oak tree. He eats away until he's completely satisfied, never once looking up to see where his food came from. How many of us fall into that category? If we do, we tend to take our blessings for granted. Doesn't everyone's family have two cars and enough food to eat? Doesn't everyone have the freedom to live and move and have our being? Don't we all have the right to life, liberty, and the pursuit of happiness? Yes, we do—at least at the present time. But are we aware that all of those blessings and liberties could one day be taken from us? At the present time we may see nothing really to complain about. Oh, we all have the usual challenges of everyday living, but nothing major to divert our attention away from the abundance and affluence we enjoy day in and day out. If we fall in this category, we are not necessarily considered complainers. We're just living a life of *simple ingratitude*.

Ingrates take their blessings for granted, and don't recognize the need to be thankful.

3. *Grateful for Obvious Blessings*. This level of gratitude probably accounts for most of us. On the scale of one to ten, I would guess that most of us, whether we are Christians or not, would register between four and eight. I have many pleasant memories of playing golf each week over the years at the Kinston Country Club, with our original foursome: Carlton Oliver, Ray Rouse, and Walker Sugg. Later, when Walker dropped out, Myron Hill joined us, and when Ray dropped out, Charlie Brown came on board. All of us appreciated the privilege of being together and enjoying the beautiful scenery. We all were aware of these obvious blessings, and expressed our gratitude to God for His grace and mercy. For more than twenty years

Carlton and I were partners and rode together. On almost every hole we would talk about the beautiful greens, the picturesque setting of fairways, ponds, and traps. Even the much-dreaded wooded areas and ditches added their touch of class to the much-appreciated overall scenery. Many times I would kid Carlton by remarking, "Have you thanked the Lord today for this beautiful course and the privilege we have of playing together?" He would come back with, "I sure have. We are so blessed!" In later years Jim Smith or Frazier Bruton and I would play Falling Creek as a twosome. There again I couldn't help but exclaim quite frequently, "Isn't this beautiful? Do you realize how blessed we are?" A few weeks ago Myron Hill and I were playing at Falling Creek with our Jewish friend Aubrey Bronstein, who had just recently returned to play after several weeks of sickness. His gratitude was exuberant when I asked him how he was doing. He kept saying how thankful he was to be able to get back to playing. I commended him for his attitude of gratitude and the fact that he was counting his blessings. Although Aubrey is not a Christian, he recognizes that he has indeed been blessed and that his blessings come from God.

It's easy to be thankful when things are going well and our blessings are obvious.

4. *Thankful—Always—In All Things*. This is considered the highest level of gratitude, or a ten on our gratitude scale. We might call it the Bible level of gratitude. If we can categorize ourselves as being in level four we have caught on to what God's Word teaches about this highest form of gratitude. It means we have reached the point in our spiritual lives where we can be truly thankful in the midst of all our circumstances. Paul plainly said, "In everything give thanks; for this is the will of God in Christ Jesus for you" (1 Thessalonians 5:18). What does he mean by "in everything give thanks"? In writing to the Ephesians Paul used similar words: "Giving thanks always

for all things unto God the Father in the name of our Lord Jesus Christ" (Ephesians 5:20).

It's interesting to note that Paul wrote those words while in prison. As a matter of fact, each of his letters to the Ephesians, Philippians, and Colossians, as well as to Philemon, are sometimes referred to the Prison Epistles, for they were all written during Paul's Roman imprisonment. To the Philippians he wrote, "Not that I speak in regard to need, for I have learned in whatever state I am to be content" (Philippians 4:11). How could he be content in prison with all its restrictions and demands? Paul learned that his contentment was in the Lord. His secret of such contentment is found in Philippians 4:13: "I can do all things through Christ who strengthens me."

Paul's deep awareness of Christ's indwelling presence and power within led him to write, "And my God shall supply all your needs according to His riches in glory by Christ Jesus" (Philippians 4:19).

A good example of level 10 gratitude is Margaret's eighty-nine-year-old sister Carolyn Hodges. She has several medical issues necessitating live-in, round-the-clock help. Carolyn never complains of her restricted living conditions. To the contrary, when we have her over for supper on Monday nights, she spends most of her time complimenting Margaret for being such a good cook and making such comments as: "I'm so blessed! I don't hurt anywhere. I just don't understand it! I have caring neighbors, many friends, and two children who love me. I'm so blessed to have Sharon and Kay from Silver Care looking after me;" and then she goes on and on counting her blessings. She loves her church and is a real inspiration to Margaret and me.

The highest level of gratitude is not *seasonal* nor is it *situational*. It is not to be practiced just on Thanksgiving Day or when things are going well. Our attitude of gratitude should characterize our whole life at all times, even in those dark days of pain and sorrow we all experience.

CHAPTER IV

The Ultimate Level of Gratitude

We have just described what I consider the four levels of gratitude. Now I'm suggesting one further level, even beyond a ten! We'll go one step beyond the highest level by calling this the *ultimate level of gratitude*. In my thinking we just can't get any higher than this. It's the pinnacle, the top of the line. You've blown the top off the scale! Why do we call this the ultimate level of gratitude? Read on.

Sometime in the early 1970s, Merlin Carothers came to Kinston to speak to a group of Christians. He revolutionized our thinking about praise and thanksgiving. His best-selling book *Prison to Praise* was the talk of the town. He had been a chaplain in the army and was a highly sought-after speaker. His basic message to us—in fact, the whole thrust of his ministry—was (and still is) that praising God is the key ingredient to a joyful and effective Christian life. He told us that he had learned not only to praise and give thanks to God *in everything*, but also *for everything*.

Should We Be Thankful for Everything?

Let's review and compare the two well-known pertinent Scripture passages that we previously mentioned:

- **1 Thessalonians 5:18**: "*In everything* give thanks; for this is the will of God in Christ Jesus for you."
- **Ephesians 5:20**: "Giving thanks always *for all things* to God the Father in the name of our Lord Jesus Christ."

These Scriptures can be confusing and even turn some people off. I believe the key thought is that God has to reveal the truth to each reader at a particular stage of his own spiritual development.

First Thessalonians tells us to give thanks *in everything*, but Ephesians goes a step further and is telling us to give thanks *for everything*.

Giving thanks *for* all things can be troubling to all of us in certain instances. I've heard it discussed many times, and even the footnotes in my New Living Translation Bible for both verses go so far as to say that Paul was not teaching that we should thank God *for* everything that happens to us, but give thanks *in* everything. They say that "Evil does not come from God, so we should not be thankful for it. But when evil strikes we can still be thankful for God's presence and for the good that He will accomplish through the distress."

We all find it difficult to give thanks during extremely dark times of adversity. Our tendency is to feel down and out and even depressed and despondent. How can we be thankful and praise God under those conditions? Merlin Carothers says that those are the very times we should praise the Lord and be thankful. We don't feel like it, but he says to do it anyway! He said, "That's what I learned to do, and it works for me." Among his many books he has written in addition to *Prison to Praise*, I recall *Answers to Praise*, *Praise Works*, and *Power in Praise*. They are all filled with stirring testimonies of how God uses the praise of believers during times of adversity to bring about blessings to the person, as well as glory to God.

The Bible Says Be Thankful for Everything

Obviously, I'm no seasoned theologian. Nor do I want to appear presumptive when I disagree with the translation committee that wrote the footnotes for the NLT Bible. On the other hand, I tend to agree with Carothers when he says he has learned to praise God *for everything*. Even though in Ephesians 5:20 the NLT uses the words, "and gives thanks for everything to God," the committee writing the footnote says, "Thank God, not for your problems but for the strength He is building in you through the difficult experiences in your life. You can be sure God's perfect love will see you through."

Although most people I know may agree with the footnotes, that is not what the verse says. The committee's interpretation appears to me to be a direct contradiction to what the words of the Bible actually say. The matter came up in one of our Bible studies last year, and one lady explained that she simply cannot thank God **for** the "really bad" things that happen to her and her family. She says she can praise Him in the midst of the adversities, even while they are happening, but she simply cannot thank Him for them.

Why We Can Thank God for Our Adversities

At first glance I'm sure many of you will disagree with my conclusion that we can find a way to thank God *for* all our adversities no matter how tragic the situation. Hang on now. Don't give up on me. Please remember that we're talking about the *ultimate* level of gratitude. Few find it. Personally, I'm far from being there, but I'm working on it.

I know it can be confusing, and even turn some people completely off, but I think the answer can be found in the phrase, "...for this is the will of God in Christ Jesus **for you**" (1 Thessalonians 5:18). That's the key! If we are to understand this mystery of the Word, God in His sovereignty must reveal it to us. We should keep in mind that each Christian reader is at a different stage of growth and development in his Christian life. In other words, to some this truth may be revealed, and to others it may not.

I'm persuaded of three basic reasons that *some believers in Jesus Christ can indeed be led to thank God for all their adversities*. I'm further persuaded that we must look beyond all human reasoning and with the Lord's help try to see every situation, every circumstance, from God's perspective. If we are to be able to thank God *for all things*, we must trust implicitly in these three Biblical principles:

1. **Trust in God's Word.** In this instance God's Word clearly says, "Giving thanks always *for all things* to God" (Ephesians 5:18). Every translation I've looked at uses the words "for all things": the Authorized King James Version, the New King James Version, the Modern Language translation, Eugene Patterson's *The Message*, the New Testament in Modern English, the New Living Translation, and the Living Bible (paraphrase), to name just a few. They also use the words "in all things" in 1 Thessalonians 5:20. Skeptics argue that the two verses contradict each other. I disagree.

I believe Paul is teaching two different truths: that we should not only be thankful *in all things*, but also *for all things*.

2. **Trust in God's Sovereignty.** If we can go so far as to praise God for everything that comes into our lives, we are developing a firm understanding

of the total sovereignty of God. We are developing an abiding trust that the God who created the universe is the same God who sustains it. The truth is that He is ultimately in total control not only of all the universe but also of all His created beings, whether we believe in Him or not. The rampant sin, famine, and suffering we observe all give the appearance that the world is out of control, yet the Bible is clear from Genesis through Revelation that "the Lord has made the heavens His throne; from there He rules over everything" (Psalm 103:19). It's taken me awhile to get a grip on the fact that even though God is always in control and in charge of history, in His sovereignty He has chosen to allow sin and evil, as well as all adversities, to come into the lives of His children. This leads us to the third principle of trust.

3. **Trust in God's Goodness.** Romans 8:28 is one of my favorite Bible verses, and I'm convinced beyond doubt of its absolute truth: "And we know

that God causes everything to work together for the good of those who love God and are called according to His purpose for them" (NLT). Charles Stanley uses the image of an engineer sitting behind the controls of our lives. He says, "God is engineering everything He allows to happen to us for our good." In other words, all adversities that happen to a believer who loves God will eventually turn out to be a blessing in disguise. The Modern English Version says, "Everything that happens [to a believer] fits into a pattern for good." Peterson's *The Message* says, "That's why we can be sure that every detail of our lives of love for God is worked into something good." This does not mean that everything that happens to us is good, for evil is prevalent in our world. The good news is that God can and does *cause* "everything" (including evil things) to work together for our long-range good. The bad news is that this promise is not for unbelievers, those who reject or simply have not made a deliberate decision to accept Christ.

The Bottom Line

The bottom line of the ultimate level of gratitude is *an unfaltering trust*! If we are to go so far as to be able to thank God and praise Him *for all things* as well as *in the midst of all things*, our unfaltering trust in Him is essential.

We must consistently trust in the truth of God's Word; we must trust in the reality of God's sovereignty; and we must trust in the all-encompassing goodness of our heavenly Father, for He is the God who created us and the God who wants the best for us. We must place our absolute and total trust in the fact that He is the Potter and we are His clay. We are in the hands of a loving God who is molding all of life's circumstances to work together for the good of His children.

CHAPTER V

Should We Really Thank God for All Things?

As we indicated in the last chapter, most Christians would agree with Paul in his admonishment of the Thessalonians to give thanks *in everything* that happens to them. Most of us are far enough along in our spiritual walk that we can look back at the dark times in our lives and see (after the fact) that, yes, God did indeed eventually work it all out for our good. While in the bottom of the pit, during our valley experience, we were dejected and depressed, but now in retrospect we see how it all worked out for our good. We say that the next time it happens we'll try to learn from past experience and thank Him and praise Him while actually going through the deepest valley, just like Paul says.

Let's reiterate the obvious: It's one thing to give thanks in the midst of dark times, but it's quite a different story to give thanks *for* the bad things while we are experiencing them. We argue that to praise God and actually thank Him *for* allowing bad things to happen to us is asking too much. We rationalize that He could not have meant for us literally to thank Him *for* certain tragedies that have happened throughout the world and in our personal lives. How can we thank Him for a broken marriage or when a daughter is raped or a little child is beaten and abused? How can we thank God for the holocaust and the mass massacre at Columbine? Even in the light of God's Word, this is troubling to all of us.

But let's read once again Paul's words to the Ephesians put in context with the previous two verses:

> But be filled with the Spirit, speaking to one another in psalms and hymns and spiritual hymns,

singing and making melody in your heart to the Lord, *giving thanks always for all things* to God the Father in the name of our Lord Jesus Christ (5:18–20).

My Personal Testimony

One of the most earth-shattering things that happened in my life was failing the North Carolina Bar exam in 1958 when I was fresh out of law school. In our law class at Carolina there were only two who failed, and I was one of them. I had never failed at anything before, for my life had always run smoothly with very few, if any, real hitches along the way. I will never forget the deep feeling of disappointment and frustrating defeat when Daddy broke the news to me. Even though I sensed his obvious disappointment, he and the rest of my family and friends were all supportive and encouraging. They assured me it was not the end of the world and I would have another day (next year) to prove I could do it. Although I was not far enough along in my spiritual journey to praise God and thank Him *for* this valley experience, or even praise Him *in the midst* of it, somehow I knew in my heart that the Lord would work it all out for my good. You might say I knew enough to claim the truth of Romans 8:28 and even 1 Thessalonians 5:18 (*in* all things) but not enough to go so far as to affirm Ephesians 5:20 (*for* all things). The good news is that my "failure" in no way affected my one-year job as research assistant for Justice R. Hunt Parker of the North Carolina Supreme Court. The further good news is that the following August, I succeeded in passing the bar. I went on to have a rewarding career in practicing law, first in Chapel Hill for twenty-seven months, then moving to Kinston to practice with Daddy and brother Warren. The Lord knew what He was doing. He gave me an extra bonus: He taught me a great lesson in humility, as well as in trusting Him as my sovereign God. It wasn't until forty years later, however, that God began to teach me my greatest lesson in gratitude. It set me on a new course of discovering the deeper meaning of the fact that He is indeed sovereign over my life and in control of it.

My Triple "Thorn in the Flesh"

In 2008 it took three major medical occurrences (actually there were four) to get my attention: three of my own and one of Margaret's. Margaret and I were moving along pretty well with our times of meditation and Bible study. We thought we were making at least decent progress in developing a closer relationship with our heavenly Father and understanding the work of the Holy Spirit within us. But apparently the Lord wanted to lead us deeper and teach us more about dealing with adversity. *He had to give Margaret a thorn in the flesh and give me a triple thorn in the flesh to wake us up and get our attention.* He wanted to teach us what the ultimate level of gratitude was all about.

In June 2008 Margaret broke her leg in a freak accident in Statesville at a wedding luncheon for my nephew Stockton Perry and Page Spencer, his bride-to-be. Under crowded conditions Margaret fell backward into an indoor swimming pool. It was a bad break and resulted in three orthopedic surgeries. During that same time frame, I had a torn left rotator cuff as well as a severe case of shingles in the same shoulder and arm. On top of that, I was experiencing an acute attack of eczema that resulted in large red blotches all over my body. Needless to say, with all that going on I was experiencing the deepest valley of my life.

The Lord Wanted to Teach Me Something

In *My Greatest Discovery… Christ in You, the Hope of Glory*, I devoted three chapters to Margaret's and my thorns in the flesh and the many things we learned from them. For the purposes of this book I'll only zero in on what the Lord was teaching me about gratitude and why I could be thankful **for** the pain and agony I went through. I use the word "agony" because that's exactly how I can best describe the excruciating pain I experienced, especially during the deepest level of intensity. Maybe the Lord wanted me to get a glimpse of what women go through in childbirth. Only a mother can identify with the excruciating intensity and the uncontrollable outburst of emotions that the birth process entails.

During my time of deepest misery I was led to remember how Merlin Carothers learned to thank God in and for all things. As trite as it may sound, he said the hardest thing he ever had to do was get out of bed in the morning. He loved to sleep and lounge in the bed. He put off getting out of bed time and time again. "Just give me another minute" was his mind-set. He was a great procrastinator when it came to getting up in the morning. I'm sure most all of us can identify with that at least to some degree.

But one particular morning God revealed to him these thoughts:

> Okay, Merlin, I know it's hard for you to get up. I'll go along with your griping and grumbling, but only upon one condition, and that is this: If you can honestly say that your getting out of bed is harder for you than the pain and agony My Son suffered for you on the cross, then I'll let you stay in bed and gripe and grumble and complain all you want. But if it's not any tougher than what Jesus went through for you on the cross, then I want you to get on out of bed and start praising Me and thanking Me for your little insignificant problem.

Carothers said that ever since then, he's been able to thank God for all his problems—little things, big things, and yes, even tragic things. Carothers praises God *for all things* because he trusts God to work it all out for his good. The first time I heard Carothers say that was when I picked him up at the airport. On the way to our meeting we were experiencing a slight traffic jam. I was beginning to get a little irritated, but he saw through it and calmly uttered, "Praise the Lord." It was a lesson I never forgot, and it came dramatically to mind in my time of intense suffering. That was the night when the excruciating pain in my left arm and shoulder was so severe that all I could do was yell and scream! I couldn't contain myself. I tried without success not to make so much noise, but I simply couldn't help it. At that point I remembered Merlin Carothers, as well as Jesus on the cross. I caught myself literally screaming repeatedly, "Thank You, Lord! Thank You, Lord! Thank You, Lord! Thank You for this pain I'm going through, for I know it's nothing, absolutely nothing compared to the pain and agony You went through on the cross for me!" As I focused my attention on Jesus and His suffering on the cross, I found a certain measure of comfort and relief for my personal situation. Even though the pain was still there, my endurance level was enhanced and heightened to the point where it became more bearable.

From that humbling experience the Lord was teaching me to trust Him more. He wanted me to look beyond my physical and mental hardship to see the future blessing He would provide. He wanted to strengthen my faith and cause me to trust Him to work it all out for my good—just like He promised in Romans 8:28. He wanted me (and Margaret) to learn to praise Him and thank Him *for* allowing me (us) to go through this dark time in our lives. I certainly haven't mastered that thought process completely, for He's still working with me in this area.

Like most if not all of you, I continue to find it difficult to thank God for certain things, especially if they involve extreme disaster and tragically affect my family.

I'm still struggling with Ephesians 5:20. But I'm also trusting that one day the Lord will reveal the truth to me so that my mind will eventually be settled.

Jesus made it clear that "the Scriptures can not be altered" (John 10:35). It therefore remains our calling to accept what His Word says, and pray that He will, in His perfect timing, enlighten our understanding so as to reveal the truth to all who earnestly seek to know Him and His Son, Jesus, who is the *Truth* (see John 14:6).

Somewhere in the muddy water of the question, the truth of God's sovereign and providential hand reigns supreme. Somehow, I believe He wants us to look beyond our present adversities, no matter how tragic, to see His causing even the worst of circumstances to work together eventually for the good of His children. I am limited in my view now, but I'm trusting that someday I will see and understand the full picture. That's also my prayer for you, dear reader, for I know that many of you are experiencing extreme tragedy and unbearable circumstances—or at least they seem that way from your limited perspective.

The challenge for all us believers is to pray that the Lord will give us the wisdom, discernment, and revelation to see all our adversities and dark times from His viewpoint and perspective. When we look beyond our present circumstances to see what He's really up to, we will find His peace and contentment in the midst of the storm. That's what Paul was able to do, and that is what you and I can do, too—if only we trust in His overall sovereignty.

CHAPTER VI

The Entire Universe Is to Praise God

If you have ever spent much time in reading the book of Psalms, you will realize that many of the psalms are devoted to prayer, praise, and gratitude to the Creator God of the universe. The psalmists emphasize God's sovereignty and the fact that as Creator and Sustainer of the universe He is in charge of history and in control of our lives and all that goes on in the world about us. We may wonder why He allows evil things to happen and why bad things happen to good people. We also wonder why evil people seem to prosper, while good and innocent people suffer beyond their deserving. A lot of this is beyond our limited power to understand. On the human level it just doesn't make any sense. How can a good God allow such evil things to happen? Yet the writers of the psalms tell us that we, as humans, are designed to give praise to our Creator. The interesting thing is that in addition to all of us humans, the psalms and other Scriptures also tell us that all of creation, meaning the entire universe, is also designed to praise Him!

The Hallelujah Psalms

The last five psalms, Psalms 146–150, have been referred to as "the hallelujah Psalms." Since the word "hallelujah" is synonymous with "praise the Lord," they are also known as "the praise the Lord psalms." It is interesting to note that each of these five psalms begins and ends with the words, "Praise the Lord!"

David Jeremiah has commented that the poet Milton believed that Adam and Eve would sing praises to God as their morning devotion when they lived in the Garden of Eden. When we read Psalm 148 it is easy to see how Milton could reach such a conclusion. It is such a beautifully written picture of the entire universe praising God, responding to His majesty and power and goodness, and returning praise to Him as its Creator.

A Close Look at Psalm 148

It may seem strange that since God created the universe, the universe with all of its inanimate facets was designed to give praise back to the Lord of all creation. How can inanimate objects praise the Lord?

This special psalm of praise is composed of fourteen verses, and is divided into two stanzas: verses 1–6 are praising the Lord from the heavens, while verses 7–14 are praising the Lord from the earth. I had never given much thought to heaven and earth actually praising the Lord until I paid closer attention to Psalm 148.

Notice the varied elements in the heavens that are praising the Lord in verses 1–6:

> Praise the Lord from the heavens;
> Praise Him from the heights!
> Praise Him, all the angels;

> Praise Him, all His hosts!
> Praise Him, sun and moon;
> Praise Him, all you stars of light!
> Praise Him, you heavens of heavens,
> And you waters above the heavens!
> Let them praise the name of the Lord,
> For He commanded and they were created.
> He has also established them forever and ever.

What a glorious picture we see of all aspects of the heavens fulfilling their intended purpose of praising God. It's beyond our limited comprehension to feature and understand how beginning at the zenith of the universe, the *heavens* and the *heights*, the *angelic hosts*, the *sun and moon and stars*, and even the *water above the heavens* are all blending into one symphony of praise to the God who created them.

Now let's look at verses 7–14 and observe how all aspects of the earth *below* the heavens are also praising their creator God:

> Praise the Lord from the earth,
> you great creatures and all the depths;
> Fire and hail, snow and clouds,

> storm and wind, fulfilling His Word;
> Mountains and all hills; fruitful trees and all cedars;
> Beasts and all cattle; creeping things and flying fowl;
> Kings of the earth and all people;
> Princes and all judges of the earth;
> Both young men and maidens; old men and children.
> Let them praise the name of the Lord,
> For His name alone is exalted;
> His glory is above the earth and heaven,
> And He has exalted the horn of His people,
> The praise of all His saints—
> Of the children of Israel, a people near to Him.
> Praise the Lord!

It's staggering to the imagination to consider the whole universe, with its complexity and various dimensions, all praising our Creator God as a part of the symphonic universal orchestra and choir.

David Jeremiah says that Psalm 148 is a picture of what is going to happen someday in the future. It is poetry, but it is also prophecy. There is coming a day when the Lord Himself is to be King over all the earth and the whole universe shall praise Him. What we are seeing here in poetry will then become reality.

CHAPTER VII

Don't Be Embarrassed by the Truth

Have you ever been riding along and suddenly you see a roadside sign saying, "Jesus Is the Way, the Truth, and the Life," or "Jesus Saves," or "Are You Saved?" Years ago we used to see such signs more than we do now. Today we do come upon an occasional bumper sticker with the same or similar words. If you are like I was in my younger days, you were turned off to the point of thinking, *To display a sign or bumper sticker like that, you've got to be some kind of kook or fanatic! It's just not normal to be talking openly about Jesus and salvation and being saved from our sins. It may be okay*

in a church setting—but certainly not in public. It's a private thing and not something to be mentioned or displayed in the public arena.

After I came to know Jesus in a real way, my perception of such comments became more normal than fanatical. The bottom line is that God was using those roadside signs to help me understand the truth, that Jesus is indeed the Way, the Truth, and the Life, and according to God's Word He is *the only way* by which we can be saved from our sins. In testifying before Annas the High Priest and others, the Apostle Peter explained, "Nor is there salvation in any other, for there is no other name [than Jesus] under heaven given among men by which we must be saved" (Acts 4:12).

Being Saved from Your Sins Is Not Complicated

A lot of people may think that being saved from our sins involves a complicated system of doing a certain number of good works.

The truth is that salvation has nothing to do with our performance. It has nothing to do with what we have to do. It's based totally on what Christ has already done for us some two thousand years ago!

Christ's death on the cross was the ultimate price for our sin debt by the shedding of His blood for us. As the Perfect Lamb of God He was the Perfect Sacrifice. Because we are a sinful people we are not qualified to pay our own sin debt. In other words, He knew we couldn't pay, so He paid for it us.

This often-quoted statement of His grace and mercy is true:

> He paid a debt He did not owe;
> We owed a debt we could not pay.

No good works are required of us for our salvation, but we do need to understand that we were saved "*for* good works" (Ephesians 2:19). So if it's not by good works, how then are we saved? In Acts 16:30–31 the keeper of the prison in charge of Paul and Silas asked that same question: "Sirs, what must I do to be saved?" The Scripture records their answer: "Believe on the Lord Jesus Christ and you will be saved, you and your household." It's a simple matter of our faith, and not our works or performance. Ephesians 2:8 makes it clear that we are saved by God's grace through our faith alone in Jesus and His blood sacrifice.

The Question of the Ages

The question that will determine your eternal destiny is simply this: "Are you saved?" In other words, "Do you know Jesus as your Lord and Savior?" That is the most important question that will ever be asked of you, dear reader! If you find it in any way offensive, or if it turns you off completely, please understand that the question still remains forever before you. You cannot avoid its confrontation and consequences. We all must answer that question whether we want to or not. Many will say, "No, I'm not going to think about it, much less worry about it. I'll just go about my daily activities as if the question were not there." Friend, if that is your attitude, you have just given your answer. You have clearly proclaimed, "No, I am not saved, for I don't know Jesus as my Lord and Savior!"

By ignoring the question of God's calling, you have unwittingly rejected God's offer of salvation.

In all likelihood you have not considered the fact that upon your physical death on earth, your body will be returned to dust, but your soul will live throughout all eternity in one of two places. Revelation 20 paints a gloomy picture of eternal damnation (hell) reserved for all those who reject Jesus. According to verse 15, "And anyone not found written in the Book of Life was cast into the lake of fire." On the other hand,

Revelation 21 and 22 describe a glorious glimpse of what heaven will be like for those who accept Jesus. Believers in Jesus will live forever in God's presence and experience the indescribable blessings of eternal life. According to verse 21:7 God makes it clear that, "He who overcomes shall inherit all things, and I will be his God and He will be My son."

Amazingly enough, where we spend eternity hinges entirely on whether we are saved from our sins. If we are saved from our sins, we can be forever thankful for Jesus—and we can well understand why Oswald Chambers so wisely wrote, "The thing that awakens the deepest well of gratitude in a human being is that God has forgiven sin."

PART TWO

Responding to Others With Gratitude and Appreciation

CHAPTER VIII

The Perspective of Gratitude and Glorifying God

Recently I read an article by Marcia Perkins-Reed. Even though I didn't see anything to indicate that she was a Christian, she makes an interesting distinction between gratitude and thankfulness. She writes, "Gratitude comprises more than simply being thankful. Thankfulness is directed toward a specific object or event that has just happened, as in 'I am thankful for the new sweater I just received.' Gratitude, by contrast, is a lifestyle—a way of living." She goes on to explain, "People who live *in a state of gratitude* have developed the ability to embody, moment by moment, a sense of wonder and contentment with their lives just as they are. And as they do so, they paradoxically seem to attract more and more blessings into their lives in the form of money, fulfilling jobs, deeply satisfying personal relationships, and other things that they desire." I think she makes an interesting observation, for she concludes that when we express thankfulness on a regular basis we are led to live a gratitude-filled lifestyle. However, I take issue with her statement in two ways:

First, we are left with the impression that if we live in a state of gratitude to God, He will automatically give us the material blessings we desire.

Second, she does not address the issue of the person who has a humble, grateful heart but does not experience the obvious worldly blessings she describes. That's when the Lord blesses us in other ways beyond our surface understanding—sometimes in ways that don't appear in the form of what we normally think of as blessings. We may never see the answers to some of our prayers on this side of eternity. See Hebrews 11:35–39. That's when we are called to trust that God's ways and thoughts are higher than our ways and thoughts, as described by the prophet Isaiah. Listen to what he wrote:

> "My thoughts are nothing like your thoughts," says the Lord. "And My ways are far beyond anything you could imagine. For just as the heavens are higher than the earth, so My ways are higher than your ways and My thoughts higher than your thoughts." (Isaiah 55:8–9, NLT)

God does not expect us, nor does He intend for us, to understand all of His thoughts and ways, but He does want us to express our gratitude by giving Him thanks not only in all things, but for all things, merely because of who He is as Creator, Redeemer, and Author of everything we will experience as humans.

If we can extend our faith and trust to the *ultimate level*, we will have torn down perhaps the greatest barrier in our understanding of God's sovereignty.

Thanking God for All Things—Revisited

The reason a believer in Jesus Christ is to thank God for all things is that by doing so he gives all glory to God. Whether we ever receive any material blessings is not the point. Many Christians throughout the world are experiencing devastating persecution to a degree we can't even imagine. They are reaping no material blessing. In fact it is just the opposite! Yet, they find it in their hearts to praise God and thank Him *for who He is* in their lives.

This needs to be made clear, and all Christians must fully understand: We are not to thank God for all things, believing that He will be obligated to shower us with all the things we desire. I find nothing in the Scriptures to support such a notion. Keep in mind, however, that Psalm 37:4 does say, "Delight yourself also in the Lord, and He shall give you the desires of your heart." To delight in the Lord means to experience great joy by just being in God's presence. The better we know Him and the more we understand what Jesus did for us on the cross, the more we will take delight in the Lord by just being in His presence.

The context of the entire Word of God, and especially the Psalms, is that we are to thank and praise God *for who He is*, thereby giving Him glory for what He has already done for us. We are to thank Him for how He is working to bring good out of every situation that comes our way. Psalm 147:1 says, "Praise the Lord! For it is good to sing praises to our God, for it is pleasant and praise is beautiful."

We Are to Glorify God in All Things

Everything we do should bring glory to God. It's all about Him and not us. Two Scriptures come to mind:

- "Therefore, whether you eat or drink, or whatever you do, do all to the glory of God" (1 Corinthians 10:31).
- "And whatever you do, do it heartily, as to the Lord and not to men" (Colossians 3:23).

One of my mentors is Erwin Lutzer, who has served as pastor of the Moody Church in Chicago since 1980. He says that each morning he prays this simple prayer: "Father, glorify Yourself in my life at my expense." That says it all. That should be the prayer and life's purpose of all of us. We would then be confirming the Shorter Westminster Catechism, which states that the chief aim of man is to "glorify God and enjoy Him forever."

Beware of the "Prosperity Gospel"

Many people watch preachers or teachers on TV who tell them that if they will send money or certain items to the preacher, the Lord will bless them in both material and immaterial ways. This is teaching a "prosperity gospel," and we need to be careful before we move too far in that direction. Although the Bible does teach "We reap what we sow" (see Galatians 6:7), we need to put that teaching in proper context.

It is a pagan idea to think that
if I give to God, He will give me
what I want (or think I need).

It goes back to the detestable Old Testament pagan practice of sacrificing children to false "gods." That, along with the present prosperity gospel, is totally opposed to the biblical principle of doing everything for the glory of God. The popular TV personality Joel Osteen is among the leaders of the positive-thinking prosperity gospel. Although he is well received in many circles as an encourager and "feel-good-about-yourself" motivational speaker, I do think that we need to be careful before we accept everything he says as biblically true.

We Can Learn from Job

If we study the book of Job we can learn some valuable lessons about our relationship with our sovereign God and how He allows suffering to glorify Him. God allowed Satan to cause Job unbearable suffering. One day Job had all the blessings God could give him: family, friends, wealth, health, and respect by all. Within a matter of a day or two, he had lost it all! The point is that through his suffering and discouragement, Job did not turn his back on God even though he reached the point of wanting to die. Job did, however, question over and over again, why did God allow such suffering in his life? He was a man whom God considered "a blameless and upright man who fears God and shuns evil ... and holds fast to his integrity" (Job 2:3). He simply did not understand why.

God answered with a series of questions, all designed to redirect Job's attention away from his own questioning plight and on to God's sovereign control:

> Where were you when I laid the foundations of the earth? Tell me if you have understanding. Who determined its measurements? Surely you know! Or who stretched the line upon it? To what were its foundations fastened? Or who laid its cornerstone, when the morning stars sang together, and all the sons of God shouted for joy? (Job 38:4–7)

God's questioning of Job continues for a total of sixty-seven verses through Job 39:30, and then concludes with this final question and suggested answer:

> Moreover the Lord answered Job, and said: "Shall the one who contends with the Almighty correct

> *Him*? He who rebukes God, let him answer it."
> (Job 40:1–2)

That was God's way of putting in perspective Job's questioning of *why* he was allowed to suffer. In essence God was saying, "Who do you think you are? Where were you when I created the world and all its creatures?" Job finally came to his senses and realized how great God is and how all glory belongs to Him.

God deserves all
glory, honor, and praise,
not because of what
He does or doesn't give,
but *because of who He is*!

CHAPTER IX

Saying "Thank You" Is a Rewarding Experience

Many people have advocated that saying "thank you" can be one of life's most enriching moments. David Jeremiah challenges us with the question, "Is there someone I need to thank before Christ returns?" In his pamphlet *7 Days until Christ Returns*, he emphasizes that today is the day to say "thank you."

Jeremiah quotes Dr. Robert A. Emmons, professor at the University of California at Davis, who for many years has studied the subject of saying "thank you." In his book *Thanks! How Practicing Gratitude Can Make You Happier*, he wrote, "Our groundbreaking research has shown that grateful people experience higher levels of positive emotions such as joy, enthusiasm, love, happiness, and optimism, and that the practice of gratitude as a discipline protects a person from the destructive impulses of envy and resentment, greed, and bitterness."

It's such a simple yet often neglected thing to do, to utter those two words to someone who befriends us during the day. Sometimes a thank-you card or special letter is called for. At other times an unexpected phone call or visit will serve the meaningful and uplifting purpose of expressing gratitude to someone who has affected our lives.

You Can Always Find Someone to Thank

Most of us don't take time to focus our attention on finding someone to thank, unless it's for a big favor, birthday present, or the like. Let's consider just four areas or categories of people to thank:

1. **Someone in your past.** All of us have people who have had a positive influence on our lives. I

recently read that a group from Harvard University had launched an annual "Thank Your Mentor" day, encouraging students to reach out to honor and thank those who have encouraged and influenced them in some significant way. That's a good exercise all of us should practice—and not wait to start. Most of us can pinpoint one or more teachers who have had a lasting influence on our lives, some more than others, some for what they say, others for the example they set for us. We remember them and think about them often, but have we ever really thanked them? I remember most all of my grammar school teachers at Harvey School: Mrs. Guthrie (first grade), Mrs. Marston (second grade), Mrs. Benthal (Rasberry) (third grade), Miss Hooker (fourth grade), Miss Lanier (fifth grade), and Miss Fletcher (sixth grade); also Mrs. Fay (art and drawing), Mrs. Cobb (literature), and Miss Scarborough (arithmetic). All of them are dead now, and I believe the only one I ever wrote was Miss Fletcher when I heard she was dying of cancer.

> The point is, most of our teachers impact our lives in some positive way, and we should take the time to say "Thank you."

I am reminded of a little poem I've often quoted:

In this world of hurry and work and sudden end,
If a thought comes quick of doing a kindness to
  a friend,
Do it this very instant!
Don't put it off, don't wait!
What's the use of doing a kindness,
If you do it a day too late!

Being that I'm eighty years old now, I assume that all of my teachers at Grainger High School as well as Woodberry Forest are deceased, except Blair Gammon. Blair was my special tutor in first-year Spanish in summer school 1946 when I was trying to get into Woodberry as a fourth-former (sophomore).

His patience and encouragement paved the way for my being accepted and to go on to have a rewarding three-year experience at Woodberry. In my senior year Blair was my basketball coach who led us to the state championship in the Prep School League in the state of Virginia. Some time ago I renewed my friendship with Blair with a two-night visit to his home in Charlottesville, as well as with frequent telephone calls. A few months ago I wrote him a special thank-you letter. He is eighty-five and legally blind. Although I have thanked him personally and even written about him in several of my books, I just wanted him to know once more how much I appreciate him and the profound impact he has had on my life.

2. **Someone in your family.** Sometimes our mother or father, or an aunt or uncle, is the last person we remember to thank. Maybe we just never get around to it. It could be that we rationalize that they already know that we love them and appreciate all they've done for us, so why do we need to thank them? Why would an elderly grandmother

or grandfather need to be thanked? Let me suggest that no one is beyond appreciating a simple thank-you. We all like to be remembered and thanked for the little things in life as well as the big occasions. It brings to mind the story of the rough-and-tough red neck when asked by his marriage counselor if he ever told his wife he loved her. In response he flat out made it clear, "I told that woman when I married her that I loved her and if I ever changed my mind I'd let her know!" That may hit closer to home than some would care to admit, but sometimes we tend to overlook the need to tell a spouse or child we love them and appreciate their little acts of kindness, when they're the ones who need it the most.

I remember writing my uncle, Dr. Clifton F. West, a thank-you letter for all his many years of doctoring me since childbirth. In fact, he delivered me and attended to my every medical need right on up to the time shortly before his death when I was in my forties. The same was true with my entire family. He looked after all the Perrys without charge in exchange for free legal services rendered by my father, and later by my brother Warren. His unselfish, dedicated, and capable medical service was appreciated by us all, but I'm not so sure I thanked him every time before leaving his office, especially in my younger years. In any event, I'm so glad I wrote that letter before he died. I likewise appreciated his kind and gracious response.

3. **Someone who has served in the military.** On December 24, 1954, I shipped out from Seattle to begin a sixteenth-month tour of duty in Korea in an army heavy weapons company. The peace treaty was signed on July 27, 1953, so the fighting was over. The life of a soldier was different from anything I had ever encountered; it was quite a learning experience. Most of the time I received weekly, if not daily, mail from home, so I had plenty of support, especially from Mother and other family members. One of the most memorable letters I received came from Poo Rochell's mother, Mrs. Vernabelle Rochell. It was a newsy letter full of church and hometown items that included a number of inserts, such as church bulletins

and newspaper articles. They were all comforting, but the thing that encouraged me the most was that she concluded with a simple "thank you for your service in the military." It was really touching to think that what I was doing was appreciated by people back home, especially by a non–family member.

David Jeremiah tells the story of an elementary school in Macon, Georgia, that recently called the students to the cafeteria for an assembly program. At the front of the room, a large screen was connected to Iraq via satellite, and the children were able to sing patriotic songs, wave flags, and talk to the soldiers. At one point the communication was disrupted when the sound was cut off from the students to the soldiers. The youngsters weren't to be denied. They started writing out their comments and questions, which they held up to the camera and listened for the responses. It was their way of boosting the morale of our men and women in uniform, and it worked. Jeremiah concludes, "There's no 'thanks' to compare with one coming from a child."

Most all of us know a serviceman or servicewoman stationed somewhere in the world. We also will know a veteran either in church, business, or some other capacity. But have we ever thought of writing them a little thank-you note to let them know they are appreciated? We probably don't give it much thought. We are too busy doing our own thing.

If only we could put ourselves in the other fellow's shoes, we would know how much a thank-you note means to them!

My best friend from early childhood, Z. A. Collins, was in Tokyo the same time I was in Korea, and when I was on R&R leave we were able to spend most of that time together. Of course with him being a commissioned officer, I had to give him a crisp salute when we first met. He showed me around the city as well as surrounding area, and we had a great time together for almost a week. We played golf, rode motor scooters, and even went skiing on Mount Fuji. Upon returning to Camp Casey in Korea I immediately wrote Z. A.'s daddy (Zollie) to let him know of our adventures. What he appreciated most was when I exclaimed what a great daddy he was to raise such a fine son—who took the time to show me around and have such a good time. He even got me a supper date with a colonel's daughter. My mother wrote back and said Zollie was so excited, he carried my letter with him everywhere he went and showed it to all his friends. Of course that made me feel good, but the point is, it lifted his spirits and made him proud of his son. We never know what a simple thank-you letter will do in the life of another.

4. **Someone in your church.** We can all learn a valued lesson from the Apostle Paul, who was quick to thank people who were laboring in the vineyard of the various churches he founded and visited. For instance, he wrote the church of Corinth: "I thank my God always concerning you for the grace of God which was given you by Christ Jesus" (1 Corinthians

1:3). To the Philippians he wrote, "I thank my God upon every remembrance of you" (Philippians 1:3), and to the Thessalonians he wrote, "We give thanks to God always for you all, making mention of you in our prayers, remembering without ceasing your works of faith, labor of love, and patience of hope in our Lord Jesus Christ in the sight of our God and Father" (1 Thessalonians 1:2–3).

Almost without exception, church work can be tough at times and even brutal, being little more than a complaint department for grumbling and griping members. It's easy to observe that Christians can gripe and complain more than anyone. That's why a sincere, meaningful, special word or letter of gratitude can make all the difference. There is always something good we can say about our pastors. Have you taken the time to express your appreciation for someone in the ministry, especially your own pastor, assistant pastor, or minister of music? If not, this is the day to say "thank you."

I was led to Christ and baptized by Dr. J. Wayne Drash on Easter morning 1944 as a twelve-year-old at Gordon Street Christian Church. More than forty years later I happened to see Dr. Drash at a church meeting in Greensboro shortly before his death. At that time I made a special point to thank him for leading me to Christ. I am glad the Lord opened the door for that opportunity, for I could tell he was most appreciative of my comments.

Have you found
the time to thank
the one who led you
to accept Jesus as your
Lord and Savior?

PART THREE

Practicing Gratitude as a Way of Life

CHAPTER X

Making "Thank You" a Way of Life

Many years ago when I played a lot of golf with Carlton Oliver, Ray Rouse, and Walker Sugg, on many occasions I heard Walker respond to a good shot by quietly exclaiming, "Thank You, Lord." That simple expression characterized Walker's lifestyle, but it was also a witness to all of us. Carlton, my golf-cart partner, and I would extend Walker's expression as we rode along with comments such as, "Thank You, Lord, for the beauty all around us—for the birds and trees and squirrels and clouds . . ." and on and on we would go—just being thankful for everything around us.

The two simple words, *thank you*, are more effective and profound than we might imagine. If you think about it, in that split second, there is a closeness established between you and the person you say it to. When we thank God for a particular blessing or benefit, we are responding according to His will that we give thanks in and for all things. We are therefore being drawn closer in our fellowship with Him.

When we say "thank you" to other people, we are making them feel wanted, appreciated, and important in the way they feel about themselves and their relationship with us.

You Cannot Give without Receiving

That's an amazing statement, but it's true. The learned philosophers even tell us it is a law. Someone has said, "We give what we choose, and we receive back that which we give, so, in fact, we choose what we receive in life." It's a simple truth that we should all learn. In his article, "A Short Cut to a Miracle," Rev. Michael C. Rann challenges his readers to "Try it for yourself!" He says to say "thank you" and watch for the results. Then he says, "You will be amazed by how quickly your life becomes filled with wonderful outcomes that some choose to call *miracles*." Rann makes a good point as he emphasizes what saying "thank you" does for you. He says it not only makes another person feel good, but it also makes you feel good. It then follows that when you make another person feel important, you yourself also feel important. We can all relate to our being inspired to feel good and important as well as appreciated. It's all about having an *attitude of gratitude* and saying the two simple words, "thank you." We've all heard of the adage, "You can't give good away. It keeps coming back bigger and better than when you gave it." The same is true of "thank you"s. The more you give them away, the higher the yield of return. That same principle is taught in Ecclesiastes 11:1 (NLT): "Send your grain across the seas, and in time, profits will flow back to you."

"Thank You"—The Highest Form of Prayer

Someone has said that by practicing the power of gratitude, you are practicing the highest form of prayer. That makes a lot of sense, for I believe that all of our prayers should be centered around a grateful heart, the goodness of God, and what He has done for us through the giving of His Son.

The Apostle Paul emphasized the need for expressing thanksgiving when he admonished the Philippians, "Be anxious for nothing, but in everything by prayer and supplication, *with thanksgiving*, let your requests be made known to God" (Philippians 4:6).

Likewise, the well-known acrostic, ACTS (Adoration, Confession, Thanksgiving, and Supplication) stresses the importance of thanksgiving as a guide for all prayers.

Back when I was growing up at Gordon Street Christian Church I well remember the formal, rather stilted manner of the elders as they offered their prayers at the Communion table. You might say they used the words of the old King James Version of the Bible—scattered with *Thee*s and *Thou*s and *Thy*s and *Thine*s, and all in between. That was before the more modern translations changed "Thee" and "Thou" to "You," and "Thy," and "Thine" to "Your." Most of the time the standard elder's prayer would include words similar to, "We thank Thee for Thy many blessings." But one Sunday morning I heard a noticeable change of pace. My father had recently been named an elder and was praying his first prayer at the Communion table. I don't remember the specifics of what he said, but I do remember it was different from all the usual elders' prayers. He was praying as if he was actually in a conversation with God. I didn't hear a single "Thee" or "Thou." Instead he simply referred to God as "You."

I happened to be sitting in the balcony with the young people, for I had reached the age where we were allowed to break away from the usual family seating and branch out to sit together with other youth. I can still remember the feeling of shock I had when I heard Daddy use the words "Thank You." To my knowledge he was plowing new ground. I had never heard anyone say "Thank You" to God in a public prayer. It was always, "We thank Thee."

Several years later, some of the others began using those same two words, although most of the oldtimers stuck to their usual formality.

Whatever words we use,
the idea is to have a thankful
attitude in responding to
God's goodness as well as the
goodness of others.

CHAPTER XI

An Experiment in Thanksgiving

My first experiment in thanksgiving was rendered when I was teaching the Moseley Class at Gordon Street Christian Church. The class was composed of older ladies, and I think it was in the early 1970s. Thanksgiving Day was approaching, and I wanted to do something practical as well as special to emphasize the season. I thought I'd conduct an experiment in Thanksgiving to encourage the students, as well as myself, to put into practice what I was preaching.

Here was the idea: The Sunday before Thanksgiving Day I gave each student a slip of paper about half the size of a sheet of typing paper. I came across an old copy recently and am including a reduced-in-size version so you can get an idea of the challenge I was proposing to the class:

EXPERIMENT IN THANKSGIVING

In seeking ways to develop a stronger faith and grow closer to God, I am undertaking this experiment in Thanksgiving every day for at least one week.

	SUN	MON	TUES	WED	THURS	FRI	SAT
1. Surprise someone with a "Thank You."							
2. Thank God for something I have never, until now, thanked Him for.							
3. Thank God for something about which I now am not happy.							
NOTES							

And here's the three-pronged daily challenge for you and me today:

1. **Surprise someone with a "thank you."** The idea here is to make it a total surprise! It can either be by telephone or in writing, or maybe even a surprise visit, but the key element is *surprise*! The person you are thanking has no idea or expectation of hearing from you. In the previous chapter we mentioned several areas or categories of people to thank. Let's review them briefly and add a few more to prompt your thinking:

- *Someone in your past.* A favorite teacher who has impacted your life is a perfect example. My observation is that an effective schoolteacher who has dedicated his or her life to helping develop young people into well-rounded and productive citizens most of the time receives very little in the way of recognition and expressions of gratitude from students. It could be a former coach, piano teacher, or dance instructor—or anybody in your past. There's bound to be somebody whom you've overlooked who deserves a much-welcomed pat on the back. Surprise them with a much-needed "Thank You!"

- *Someone in your family*. Offer a special surprise thank-you to your husband or wife, parent or child, brother or sister, aunt or uncle, cousin or whomever. They have meant a lot to you, but you have never really let them know how much you appreciate them. Surprise them with a sincere, long-overdue "Thank You!"
- *A long-lost friend or classmate*. Perhaps you haven't seen this person in years, or maybe you see him only from time to time. Let him know how much you appreciate his friendship. Surprise him with a special "Thank You!"
- *A public servant or government worker.* They work tirelessly on our behalf, many times with much criticism and little thanks. It could be a city councilman, a county commissioner, the postman, trash collector, policeman, highway patrolman ... the list could go on and on. There's bound to be someone you know who would appreciate being surprised with a special "Thank You!"

- *Someone in the military.* A relative or friend, or maybe even a casual acquaintance, deserves a surprise "Thank You!" which would mean more than you could ever imagine!
- *Someone in your church or civic organization.* Great Scott! I could go on and on! One category leads to another. The list is endless, limited only by the number of people you know—and from there it can be extended to people you've merely heard of either in the news or by reputation.

The point of all this is that there are countless people you can surprise with a simple but sincere phone call, a letter, or brief note, or maybe even a bouquet of flowers or small gift—just something to say "thank you."

Remember, the key to an unexpected "thank you" is to catch the person off guard. Make it a total surprise, and that is what makes it so special!

Back when the Moseley Class, including myself, was being challenged to do the Experiment in Thanksgiving, the idea was to give a surprise thank-you for seven straight days, beginning that Sunday. You'll notice on the form an empty space to write in a name for each of the seven days. At the bottom of the form was a space for any meaningful notes to be made for easy reference. I'm sure all of the class members were not able to fill up all the blocks, but at least we all had a purpose and goal. Even though the experiment may have had only limited overall success, it left a lasting impression on me, for I am still able to remember each of the areas of thanksgiving in the experiment.

2. **Thank God for something I have never, until now, thanked Him for.** If you give it some thought, there are probably countless things all around you that you accept as part of life, but you've never been prompted to actually thank God for them. We can start with the golf course. We may appreciate being able to play golf, but have we ever thanked God for

the golf cart itself? Many older golfers would not be able to play if it were not for the golf carts. We may appreciate the beautiful greens, but have we literally thanked God for the holes themselves and for the hole-punching instrument itself, and the pins and flags identifying the various holes? Have we taken time to thank God for the sand in the traps and bunkers? What about the ponds and actual water in the ponds? How about your golf clubs, balls, and tees? What about such a little thing as a ball marker or a divot repair instrument, or even the tee box markers? These are all little things, and yet a part of every golf game. Believe it or not, they all technically came from God even though they may be made by man. Have you ever thought about thanking God for the shutters on your house, or the stepladder in your garage, or the stakes for your tomato garden? What about the wheelbarrow and the hoe?

That little Thanksgiving experiment over forty years ago laid the foundation for my habit, even today, of thanking our sovereign Creator of the

Universe for the seemingly insignificant things of life. I catch myself expressing verbal thanks for the little things around me: Thank You, Lord, for that lampshade; thank You, Lord, for my socks; thank You, Lord, for my toothbrush; thank You for indoor toilets as well as pure running water; thank You, Lord, for that speed limit sign, that handrail, those beautiful clouds. Thank You for my feet and hands and eyes and clothes on my back.

Some may find such a habit amusing and others will even laugh.

I'm convinced that when we develop the habit of being grateful for *everything around us*, small and big, important and insignificant, we are establishing a grateful and thankful attitude that is well pleasing to our God, the Creator of all things great and small.

---

3. **Thank God for something about which I am now not happy.** This may be the hardest of all three challenges. How can we be thankful for things and situations that aren't making us happy? Maybe we should ask *why we should be thankful* for something about which we are not now happy.

Let me suggest three reasons that we should be thankful for our dark days and adverse circumstances:

First, *we are acknowledging God's sovereign rule in our lives.* That is one of the most important life lessons we can learn. The Bible makes it clear that, "The Lord made the heavens His throne and from there He rules over everything" (Psalm 103:19, NLT). To understand that God is sovereign and in control of the lives of each of His children is the key to overcoming fear, worry, and doubt. We go back to the example of the Potter and the clay as referenced in Jeremiah 18. God is the Potter; we are the clay. He molds us into the image of His choosing, according to His Divine Plan for our lives. He allows bad times as well as good times, sad times as well as happy times. Our job is to accept what comes our way, knowing that He will eventually work all things out for our good and His glory (see Romans 8:28).

Second, *we are acknowledging our dependency and trust in Him*. This goes along with knowing about His sovereignty. When we put all our trust in our own ability to do the task at hand, we are saying to the Potter, "I don't need You. I can do it myself; I'm in charge of my own destiny. I have a plan for my own life, and I don't need to depend on You for any help along the way." What God wants us to do is to trust Him when we are unhappy with the way things are going, and to turn our lives over to Him in total dependence on His sovereign plan for our lives. If we trust Him and depend on Him when we are not happy with our circumstances, we are being obedient to His Word: "Trust in the Lord with all your heart and lean not on your own understanding; in all your ways acknowledge Him and He shall direct your paths" (Proverbs 3:5–6).

Third, *we are acknowledging that our contentment is in Him and not our circumstances.* This is a lesson we can learn from the Apostle Paul: "For I have learned in whatever state I am in, to be content" (Philippians 4:11). He wrote those words to the believers in Philippi while he was in prison. Can you imagine being content while suffering the restrictions and inconvenience of being behind bars? What was his secret? The answer is found in Philippians 4:13: "I can do all things through Christ who strengthens me." Paul's contentment was based on his relationship with Jesus Christ, totally independent of external circumstances. You and I can find that same contentment when we develop our faith to the point where we can put our total trust in Christ while experiencing the adverse circumstances of this life. To trust Him implicitly means we are acknowledging our confidence in His sovereign ability to cause all things to work together for our good. To have that mind-set, dear reader, is positive evidence of our maturing in Christ. It is a slow, sometimes painful process, yet it should be our goal as we seek to please and worship our Lord and Savior.

Always remember, we can't do anything in our own strength. It's "Christ in you the hope of glory" (Colossians 1:27). It is He who gives us the faith. Our job is to cooperate with Him and yield to His leading by *letting* Him have His way with us.

CHAPTER XII

My Second Experiment in Thanksgiving

My second experiment in Thanksgiving is an ongoing discipline in my life today. It takes time and effort, but the dividends are beyond measure.

I got the idea from my friend Dr. Donald Henson, who died several years ago. I believe it was in the late 1960s or early 1970s that Don served as chairman of the United Way Campaign in Lenoir County. As was the usual custom, we all pitched in to rally the community to meet our goal. The thing I remember about that particular campaign was that after it was all over, Don sent all the workers an "Appreci-o-gram" to thank us for our participation in the success of our efforts. What a great idea!

Most of the time these types of thank-you notes are more or less a set form in nature, but the fact that Don wrote a personal three- or four-line message on an Appreci-o-gram made it something special for all of us. It was almost like getting a Western Union telegram. In our modern world of fax machines, Internet, and text messages, telegrams are a thing of the past, but back then receiving a telegram was a distinctive treat. And so it was with Don's Appreci-o-gram.

I never forgot it, and as I began writing this book about gratitude, I revised Don's idea for my own experimental use. On the back side of his form was a paragraph or two about expressed appreciation being one of the most powerful forces on earth. Everyone was encouraged to get in the habit of sending Appreci-o-grams by ordering them from the listed address. I ordered a hundred forms, which lasted several years. When I tried to reorder twenty-five years later, the ministry had gone out of business and the forms were no longer available. That is when I created my own form on yellow paper with a yellow mailing envelope so as to resemble the old telegram. I have reproduced here a smaller version:

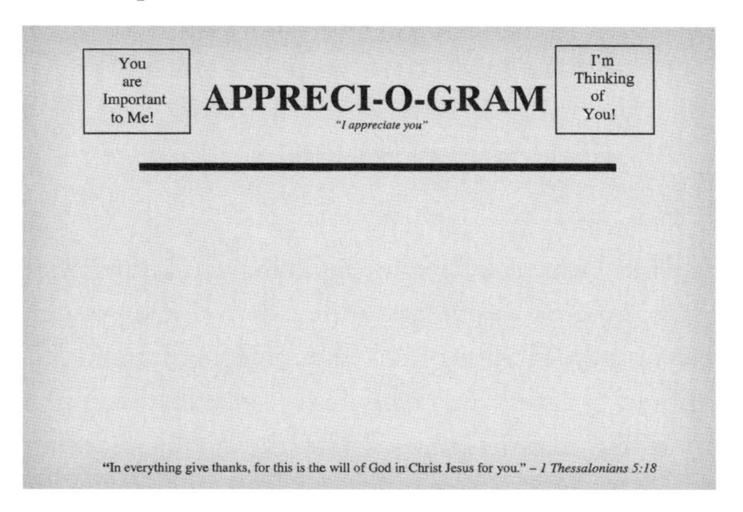

You are Important to Me!

APPRECI-O-GRAM

"I appreciate you"

I'm Thinking of You!

"In everything give thanks, for this is the will of God in Christ Jesus for you." – *1 Thessalonians 5:18*

The Essence of My Experiment

Realizing that gratitude is not thanksgiving until it is expressed, I wanted to emphasize in my own mind the importance and the need to let people know in a special way how much I really appreciate them.

We can think about it all day long, but unless we actually communicate our gratitude and make it known, how will other people ever know? It's like taking the time and effort to buy a present, wrapping it with colorful paper and ribbons, but never delivering it.

The Lord was really beginning to make it known that He wanted me to embark upon a disciplined project, maybe even a lifelong one, whereby I would send out Appreci-o-grams on a daily basis—not just on a hit-and-miss or casual basis. I had the strong yearning to get down to brass tacks and start doing it. God knew my heart, so He answered my prayer in a most unusual way. He used a book and someone else's experience to inspire me to move beyond thinking about it to actually getting it done.

365 Thank Yous

Shortly after celebrating my eightieth birthday Margaret and I were in Greenville browsing through some of the many volumes in Barnes and Noble. And then it happened! My eyes settled on a book by John Kralik interestingly titled, *365 Thank Yous*. I'm sure it was from the Lord, because it was right in line with what I knew He had been directing me to do. From the back cover I learned that it was an inspiring true story about how a simple old-fashioned act—writing thank-you notes—led a hopeless, angry middle-aged man from Pasadena, California, out of despair and into a wonderful life. I bought the book, took it home, and read it from cover to cover, underlining and making notes as I went along.

I discovered that in December 2007, at age fifty-three, John Kralik found his life at a terrible, frightening low: his small law firm was failing; he was struggling through a painful second divorce; he had grown distant from his two older children and was afraid he might lose contact with his young daughter; he was living in a tiny apartment where he froze in the winter and baked in the summer; he was forty pounds overweight; his girlfriend had just broken up with him; and his dearest life dream seemed to have slipped beyond his reach.

Then during a desperate hike on New Year's Day, John was struck by the belief that his life might become at least tolerable if, instead of focusing on what he didn't have, he could find some way to be grateful for what he had. Inspired by a beautiful, simple note his ex-girlfriend had sent to thank him for her Christmas gift, John imagined that he might find a way to feel grateful by writing thank-you notes. He set his goal—come what may—of writing 365 thank-you notes in the coming year.

One by one, day after day, he began to handwrite thank-you notes for gifts or kindnesses he'd received from loved ones and coworkers, from past business associates and current foes, from college friends and doctors, store clerks and handymen, neighbors and anyone, absolutely anyone, who'd done him a good turn, however large or small. According to his testimony, immediately after he'd sent his very first notes, significant and surprising benefits began to come John's way: financial gain, true friendship, weight loss, and inner peace. While John wrote his notes, the economy collapsed, the bank across the street from his office failed, but thank-you note by thank-you note, John's whole life turned around.

I Set a High Goal for Myself

It took John Kralik fifteen months to write his 365 thank-you notes. That's a lot of notes, but I think I can do better! In fact my goal is to write at least one Appreci-o-gram each and every day. That would be 365 Appreci-o-grams in one year. That's my goal! After the year is up, I'll reevaluate and see what I'm led to do.

Here's my report card so far: My first Appreci-o-gram went to my daughter Elizabeth on July 9, 2011, followed by son Daniel on July 10, and daughter Radford on July 11. Basically I told them how much

I love them and appreciate who they are in God's sight. As of the first 150 days—up to December 5, 2011—I had written 193 Appreci-o-grams, and I was still going strong. The good news is that I'm having a lot of fun doing it. Even though it's a discipline, I don't look at it as a burden, but more of a blessing from God each time I write one.

At first I thought I would eventually run out of names, but it now appears the more I write, the more names come to mind. It's amazing how the Lord is prompting me to find people to thank and appreciate. One person leads to another: immediate family, nephews and nieces, then cousins; then it goes from closest friends and associates to casual friends; then to people I seldom see, whether they are old classmates I haven't seen in fifty years or people I've never met. What brings me the most blessing is to surprise someone with a thank-you. The element of surprise will get 'em every time! They are blessed, and I am blessed. Most of the time I receive a phone call, note, or some other form of thank-you from the recipient, but that's not the point. Even if I never hear a word, the Lord is using this simple form of expression to bless me many times over.

Who would ever have thought that Don Henson's simple Appreci-o-gram to me over forty years ago would end up creating such a lasting ripple effect by blessing others these many years later?

Putting Appreci-o-grams in Perspective

As I relate to you my story, I am made aware that it may come across as bragging about what I have done. I pray that notion will be put in perspective with what I'm trying to accomplish here. As John Kralik's *365 Thank Yous* inspired me to venture a similar experiment of my own, so I hope it will be with you, dear reader. I'm trying to motivate you to conduct your own experiment in thanksgiving.

Even if you are led to surprise only one person with an unexpected thank-you, I'm sure it will reap benefits and blessings far beyond what you can imagine. Try it and see what happens!

CHAPTER XIII

Putting Gratitude in Perspective

We have often said that the Christian life is a life of response to God's goodness. What does it mean to live a life of response?

Responding to God's Goodness

The foundation of God's goodness is His love, His grace, and His mercy. And the foundation of His love, grace, and mercy is centered on the Cross of Calvary.

God loved the world so much that He was willing to send His only begotten Son to shed His blood and pay the ultimate price of death, so that we would not have to die spiritually. He sacrificed His life as a substitute for our life. He paid our sin debt for us by giving us His righteousness and taking our sinful nature upon Himself. He did this all because He loves us and wants us to have eternal life and live with Him forever.

We don't deserve it, but He offers us this, the greatest of all gifts, merely because He loves us. The good news is that He chose to offer this same free gift to the whole world. For those of us who respond to His goodness and grace by making the critically important decision to say, "Yes, Jesus, I accept your offer of eternal life," we are making the ultimate response to God's goodness. Such a response is the beginning of what the Christian life is all about. I'm not condemning the unbeliever, for that's not up to me. That's not my place. That's between you and the Lord.

According to God's Word . . .

Here are two appropriate Scriptures that give perspective to our response, or lack of response, to God's goodness:

- Since we believe human testimony, surely we can believe the greatest testimony that comes from God. And God has testified about His Son. All who believe in the Son of God know in their hearts that this testimony is true. Those who don't believe this are actually calling God a liar because they don't believe what God has testified about His Son. And this is what God has testified: He has given us eternal life, and this life is in His Son. Whoever has His Son has life; whoever does not have God's Son does not have life (1 John 5:9–12, NLT).

- For God did not send His Son into the world to condemn the world, but that the world through Him might be saved. He who believes in Him is not condemned; but he who does not believe is condemned already, because he has not believed in the name of the only begotten Son of God (John 3:17–18).

Responding to God Leads to Responding to Others

Once we put God's love, grace, and mercy in perspective and understand that the Christian life is a life of response to God's goodness, life really begins to be exciting! When we develop a grateful attitude and practice thanking God for His goodness in saving us from our sins, our minds become conditioned to seek out others to thank and show our appreciation. The idea is to make gratitude a way of life.

I'm convinced the Lord has led me to write these Appreci-o-grams on a continuing, constant basis. I've mentioned the element of surprise as bringing such a special blessing not only to the recipient but also to the sender. Also, when gratitude truly becomes a way of life, you enjoy looking around and searching for an answer to the questions, "Who else can I thank? Who can I thank today?" When you're constantly on the lookout for such a person, something begins to happen in your life. It might be said that you're on a roll—or at least that's the way it is with me.

By way of a further update, as of this writing on February 27, 2012, which is day 234 of my experiment, I have written 338 Appreci-o-grams. That's well ahead of my goal of 365 in one year. Some might question, why am I so obsessed with this project? Well, I guess you could call it an "obsession," but I prefer to call it what it was intended to be in the beginning: an experiment in thanksgiving. The beauty of it is that it is fulfilling its intended purpose of blessing others while enriching my own life as an added blessing. In other words, I'm having fun and being blessed while blessing others!

The whole point of this book is to help you, the reader, see the need to make gratitude your lifestyle.

My Challenge to You

If you are a Christian, I challenge you to practice thanking God each day for His grace and mercy in sending His Son to pay your sin debt in full. Thank Him for drawing you unto Himself and for giving you faith to accept Jesus as your Lord and Savior, thereby giving you eternal life, so you can live forever in His presence. Then thank Him for leading you to be consciously aware of others for whom you can show appreciation for various relationships and special acts of kindness.

If you are a believer in God, but not a believer in Christ Jesus, I still challenge you to be thankful for your many blessings and to give God the credit for providing them for you. You can and should be thankful not only to God but also to others for those little acts of kindness we all experience from time to time from family, friends, and acquaintances. The only problem is you won't be able to thank God for saving you from your sins if you have not in fact been saved. *My challenge to you* as an unbeliever in Christ Jesus is to be open-minded enough to explore your options, which are only two:

Option #1. *Accept* God's free gift of eternal life by confessing Jesus as your Lord and Savior, thereby recognizing the truth of Jesus' words when He said, "I am the way, the truth, the life. No man comes to the Father except through Me" (John 14:6).

Option #2. *Refuse to accept* Jesus as the only way to eternal life, thereby guaranteeing you *eternal separation* from the God who loves you. According to

His Word, God sent His Son to save you from your sins, thereby providing the only way for you to enter heaven and have eternal life with Him. Please keep in mind this one thing: to ignore Jesus' invitation as being the only way to eternal life is to reject it. By doing nothing, you are refusing to accept Him and, therefore, must suffer the eternal consequences.

The truth is this: Salvation is the difference between eternal life and eternal death! My prayer is that you will be wise enough to accept God's free offer and choose eternal life!

Here's One Last Challenge

Whether you are a Christian or not, I challenge you to try my Appreci-o-gram experiment.

Your obvious response is, "But I don't have any Appreci-o-grams. How can I write any if I don't have any?"

Here's the good news: Contact me, and I'll be glad to give you a starter kit to get you on your way. After that, you can either copy mine or create an Appreci-o-gram of your own. Always keep in mind: Expressed appreciation is one of the most powerful forces on earth!

A Final Thought

What if you, as you conclude this book, would purpose in your heart to develop a genuine attitude of gratitude, thereby letting gratefulness be your lifestyle each and every day? What do you think the effect would be on the world around you? What if all of us had such a lifestyle? I daresay our world would take on a totally different atmosphere, and I'm confident that you and many others would be blessed beyond what you can imagine!